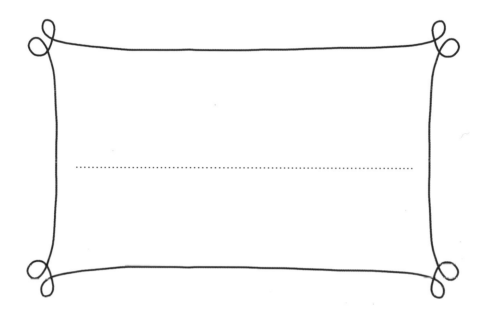

book club journal

booksandquills

Sanne Vliegenthart

has been recommending books online since 2008,
through her hugely popular Books and Quills videos.
Born in the Netherlands, she works in London as
a freelance social media producer and literary event
host. Her videos about her favourite reads, university
and publishing advice and author interviews have
been viewed by more than 15 million people. She loves
combining her years of experience working for book
publishers, including Penguin Random House UK,
with her in-depth knowledge of the online reading
world to create connections and inspire readers.

Find Sanne online at youtube.com/booksandquills
and on Instagram @booksandquills

book club journal

booksandquills

Sanne Vliegenthart

MITCHELL BEAZLEY

Contents

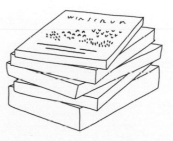

Books I've read

Here you can keep track of all the books you've read and recorded in this journal, so you can always find the page you're looking for.

1 _____
2 _____
3 _____
4 _____
5 _____
6 _____
7 _____
8 _____
9 _____
10 _____
11 _____
12 _____
13 _____
14 _____
15 _____
16 _____
17 _____
18 _____
19 _____
20 _____
21 _____
22 _____
23 _____
24 _____
25 _____

26 _____
27 _____
28 _____
29 _____
30 _____
31 _____
32 _____
33 _____
34 _____
35 _____
36 _____
37 _____
38 _____
39 _____
40 _____
41 _____
42 _____
43 _____
44 _____
45 _____
46 _____
47 _____
48 _____
49 _____
50 _____

Introduction: the joy of reading

I've been a reader all of my life, cycling to the library every week as a child, and then reading books faster than I could actually take them in – I was just so excited by how many stories were available. But not many of my friends shared this love of books and it wasn't until I went online that I found my own community of fellow readers.

Books connect us. We pass on our well-read copies, recommend them to our friends (and, let's be honest, to anyone else who is willing to listen), get lost in them and often they give rise to excellent discussion and perhaps disagreements.

Over 12 years ago, during the first year of my English degree in the Netherlands, I created my YouTube channel Books and Quills and I've been incredibly lucky to have had the chance to recommend hundreds of books to readers online, but equally I've been inspired by everyone else who shares their passion for reading with the world. From interviewing authors to working in the publishing industry and hosting book clubs that brought online readers together offline, talking about books pretty much never gets old for me.

When readers come together in book clubs, you get another chance to see different perspectives, to share a book that means a lot to you and see someone's face light up as they discuss it, but also to read something that you might have not picked up otherwise (good OR bad). Most official book clubs I've been part of have been with relative strangers, and there's something so special about meeting for the sole purpose of discussing a book you've all spent numerous hours poring over, and discovering what connects you all. There's also the unique anticipation as you wait for your friends to finish that book you recommended to them, so you can finally discuss those particular scenes you've been dying to share with someone you know.

Book clubs can also offer a bright point to look forward to, a set date that you know you'll spend with friends. And not to forget, it's an excellent motivator to put down your phone for a little bit, and properly take the time for yourself to get lost in a good book.

There never seem to be enough hours, days or even years to read all the books you want – I actually calculated how many books I'm likely to read during the rest of my life, and I wouldn't recommend doing the same – but the only solution is just to pick up the next book and turn the first page.

Whether your next book club meeting is online or in person, with old friends or new ones, remember that they're a special and beautiful opportunity, and we're so lucky to have them in our lives.

Happy reading!

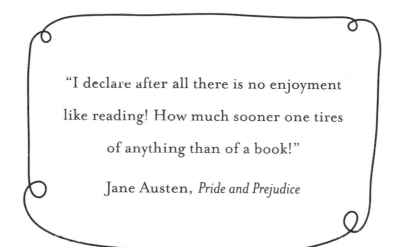

"I declare after all there is no enjoyment like reading! How much sooner one tires of anything than of a book!"

Jane Austen, *Pride and Prejudice*

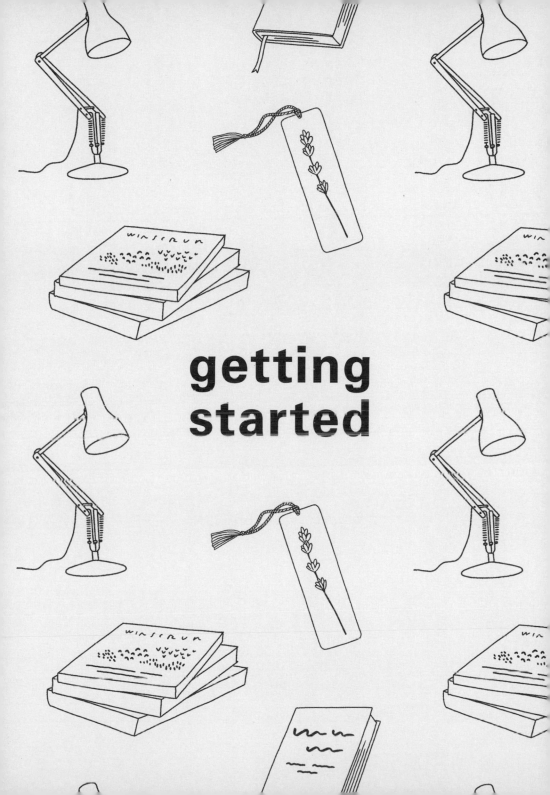

getting
started

How to navigate the dynamics of your book club

It's important to remember that no book club is the same, and there's a huge difference between creating a book club with a small group of close-knit friends versus joining one that consists of your colleagues or even total strangers. Each situation offers its own unique benefits and challenges.

The huge majority of group management boils down to the basics of making sure everyone feels comfortable and gets to share their thoughts in a safe and welcoming space. Of course there are opportunities to disagree, and for people to like or dislike the book you picked, but there are some things you should always keep in mind.

Deciding on the reading list

First of all, how do you decide which books are picked? When selecting your reads, definitely have a conversation about what the parameters are. Do you have any limits for book lengths or topics people might not feel comfortable with? Maybe you want to prioritize books you can get from the library or secondhand, to accommodate your group's budget. All of these are pretty important things to figure out beforehand, to avoid any awkward conversations when the books have been selected.

There are countless different ways to select your book. If you're taking turns and letting one person pick a book for each meeting, do remind the group (and yourself) that you want to keep the whole group in mind when picking. Your favourite 800-page sci-fi novel might not be everyone's cup of tea, so try to keep things accessible. If you want to make sure people are on board with your pick, maybe give them some comparison films or books that will get them excited (think *The Secret History* meets *Inception*!), share a moment from the book that really stuck with you when you first read it or the catchy review that made you want to pick it up in the first place.

If you're looking for a more democratic way of picking the books, why not have everyone put in three options for their choice and do an anonymous vote online? It can also be really fun to pick a theme for the month and choose titles around that. The options are endless, as long as you ensure that everyone is being heard.

How to deal with…

THE AWKWARD SILENCE

Most book clubs I've been to have started off a bit slow. This is the moment you can be extra grateful for the chatty person in the group. If you're leading the conversation, or even if you just have some topics you're keen to hear everyone's thoughts on, write them down in advance so you can whip them out and break that silence. Some great conversation starters include:

- Have you read this book before?
- Are you familiar with the author's other books?
- What were your impressions of the book before reading it?
- Which character or moment do you remember most vividly?

THE ONE WHO DIDN'T FINISH THE BOOK

A few years back I organized a one-off book club where I invited online book lovers to meet up in a bookshop. The morning of the event I started getting message after message from people saying they hadn't finished the book and weren't going to attend because of it. I managed to convince almost all of them to come along in the end, and we had an amazing discussion. I've also sat through many English Literature lectures where it was very clear that half of the students hadn't finished their assigned reading (and often I was included in that group). But after nervously making it through the lecture, I would leave feeling more intrigued and motivated to finish the book.

Long story short, if not everyone finished the book, there's no need to panic! Encourage them to come along anyway, but make sure you figure out the guidelines of your conversation. It's frequently very doable to have an in-depth discussion of the majority of the book, without revealing the ending, if needed. Every reader will bring their own experiences to the discussion, from their own life, other books they've read and, of course, however much of the book club pick they did end up reading.

If you're thinking of skipping a meeting because you didn't finish the book, keep in mind that if you do attend, you might just leave having had a lovely conversation and with a newfound inspiration to continue reading (or at the very least you now know you can pass the book on to a friend and happily dive into the next read).

THE QUIET ONE

There will always be one or more participants of your book club who might not speak up as much. Make sure to check in with them to see if they'd like to be more vocal and if there's something in particular holding them back. Of course, if they're happy being a bit quieter, that might just work out fine with your group dynamics. It's worth adding in a few low-pressure moments where everyone can chat, even if it's just a round of asking people for their first impressions to kick off the conversation and make everyone feel comfortable.

THE ONE WHO HATED THE BOOK

It's inevitable that there will be a few books that one or more people in the group will dislike. While it can be fun to totally tear down a book, do stay considerate of the person who picked it, as they obviously put it forward for a particular reason. Try to incorporate a few questions around things that everyone might have learned from the book, or perhaps other books in this genre that they did appreciate. However, if it's clear that everyone's on the same page about not liking the book, just sit back and enjoy the lively discussion!

GOING TOTALLY OFF-TOPIC

Don't feel too pressured to rein in the conversation immediately if things start going off-topic, as you're all there to have a good time. But don't hesitate to bring it up if it becomes a continuous problem and you don't get around to discussing the book at all. Often a well-placed question, especially one that continues a point someone made a few minutes ago, can get the conversation right back on track.

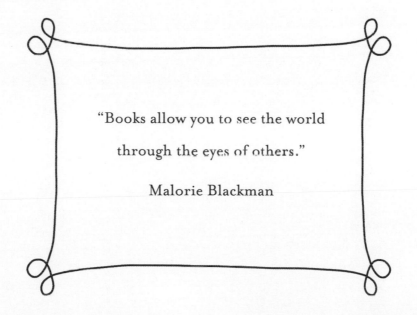

"Books allow you to see the world

through the eyes of others."

Malorie Blackman

How to read more (or, what to do if you're always running behind)

One of the biggest and most familiar fears around book clubs is the dread you feel when you know you probably won't be able to finish the book beforehand. As someone who reads at a medium pace and immediately gets reader's block when given a deadline, I'm always looking for ways to get more reading done. Here you'll find some of my long-term tried-and-tested methods.

- **Get the audiobook.** Perhaps the most obvious suggestion. I've often times swapped the print copy out for an audiobook halfway through the book, when the panic of only having a few days left to finish it sets in. Being able to read while getting your other activities done at the same time is a surefire way to catch up. Of course many books work even better in audio than print and are a great option for people who struggle with reading for a variety of reasons, so they're definitely something to bear in mind.

- **Watch the film or TV adaptation side by side while reading the book.** This is an excellent solution for any book that feels like it's moving at a glacial pace or is just difficult to follow in general. You can read a bit and then watch up to the point where you stopped reading to avoid getting spoiled for the book, while also confirming that you're on the right path with understanding what's going on. Or if you don't care about spoilers, you can watch the adaptation first (I know, shock horror!).

- **Read on your phone.** This is a hard one to convince people to do, but is a personal favourite of mine. Get whatever reading app you prefer on your phone and you'll never be without your book. Ten minutes in a queue? Waiting for the bus? Tempted to get on Instagram? Your book

is right there. I also find that reading small chunks of text at a time (because of the small screen) makes me less likely to get distracted and speeds up my reading.

- **Figure out which surrounding makes you read the most.** For a lot of people this will be a cosy reading chair, public transport or maybe a bench in your favourite park. Find what environment makes you more likely to pick up a book and try to spend more time there if you can.

- **Track your reading progress.** This is a tip for all the list and notebook lovers, who are motivated by ticking off items from their to-do list. Draw a progress bar and put it on a note next to your desk or give yourself goals of small increments on a to-do list. Sharing your thoughts and updates on your favourite social media platform can also be a handy tool, as immediate feedback or just the satisfaction of making a post can be a good motivator.

- **Give your phone to someone else.** If you can't stay away from your distractions on your own, it might be time to get serious and either get a locking app for your phone, turn it off and put it across the room or simply hand it over to someone else for safekeeping, just for the next few hours.

- **Get a reading buddy.** Find someone from your book club to read along with and hold each other accountable. Looking forward to checking in after certain markers will hopefully keep the pace going.

- **Read something else in between.** It's almost like a literary palate cleanser. Read something short and fun to rediscover the joy of reading when you find yourself stuck in a reading slump. Some poetry, a graphic novel or just the first few pages of a new book often do the trick.

- **And finally,** if you want to immerse yourself further in the book and are the kind of reader who doesn't mind listening to music, find the perfect playlist to set the scene. If that's too distracting, there are also some great ambient-sound videos with crackling fires and seaside breezes.

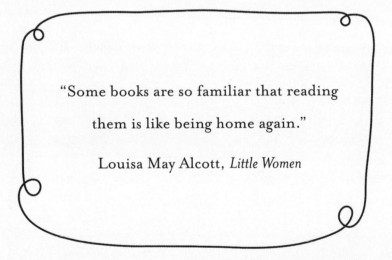

"Some books are so familiar that reading them is like being home again."

Louisa May Alcott, *Little Women*

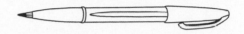

Some notes on taking notes

Do you draw a blank when trying to come up with questions and discussion points before your next book club meeting, or do you wish you had an answer to the question "what was your favourite quote from the book"? It's all in the notes! Before, during and after reading, the way you take notes will help you remember those fleeting, but brilliant thoughts you had.

Note-taking methods (the good, the bad and the ugly)

Some consider the underlining and dog-earing of books close to a crime, while others adore the sight of well-loved and scribbled-on pages. If you haven't made your choice yet, or aren't an avid note-taker, here are some options to consider:

- **Marking pages,** whether you fold corners or use slightly less destructive methods (from colour-coded sticky tabs to arrow-shaped metal page markers, my personal favourite), this is probably the most common way to keep track of your reading. No more frantically going through pages trying to retrieve that pivotal scene. This is an especially helpful method to mark question prompts if your book club discusses books one section at a time.

- **Underlining.** I love looking back at underlined sections when rereading a book and it also gives the book a lot of extra personality. You can even scribble in the margins, though personally I never feel like I have enough space. Important: don't forget to test your pens to avoid making the next page illegible because the ink has bled through. I can highly recommend using an erasable pen with a fine point.

- **Phone notes.** You're very unlikely to leave the house without a phone, so in a pinch this can be a great way to mark down some quick notes on themes, or a question that pops into your head. Then, when you sit down later to properly gather your thoughts, you'll have a base to start from.

- **Notebook/book club journal.** How handy, you've already got one of those! No need to fold corners if you're not into that and plenty of space to get your thoughts down and have them all collected in one place.

What to write down

There are some vital opportunities in the reading journey to note down your thoughts. Here are some topics and moments to keep in mind, which I've found the most useful when discussing later on:

- **Before you start reading.** You'll never get the chance again to write down your expectations about the book before reading it. So now's the time!

- **Halfway through.** Take a break and consider how you think the book might end or in which direction it will turn. This will be harder to remember once you've finished, so this is the perfect moment to take stock and write down those thoughts.

- **Characters and themes.** As you're going through the book, note down things that will be helpful to keep in mind while continuing to read. And getting those character names down is extra handy with a big cast of characters or for discussing during your book club (instead of having to refer to everyone with some vague descriptors you might remember).

- **Memorable quotes or moments.** These are the ones you'd like to recall when looking back but can be hard to find if you don't mark them.

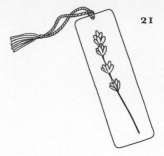

- **And finally, any questions that pop into your mind.** Perhaps confusing choices made by characters that you would love someone else's insight on, or real-life events and author queries you'd like to look into more.

While I'm in the middle of being consumed by a book I'm always convinced I'll remember everything in vivid detail, and I almost never do. So when in doubt, make a note!

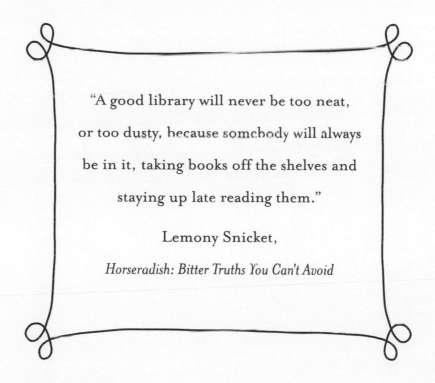

"A good library will never be too neat, or too dusty, because somebody will always be in it, taking books off the shelves and staying up late reading them."

Lemony Snicket,

Horseradish: Bitter Truths You Can't Avoid

Doing the research (or not)

There's lots to be said for going into a book club discussion without having read anything further about the book, but I'm often tempted to look up more. It's a difficult but also fairly straightforward decision: do you want to be the one with all the facts, or the one asking questions and sharing your own experiences? It all depends on what role you enjoy more, but remember that if you do choose to go full in on the background, you should also leave space for speculation and other interpretations. Anyone who's been in any sort of literature class knows how easy it is to suck the enjoyment out of reading by over-analysing, and by trying to find the "right" interpretation. But for others it's the best part of reading. It's not all black and white, but it's worth thinking about whether doing further reading will influence your experience overall. If you do want to do some background research, these are my suggestions:

- **Author interviews and videos,** especially ones about what inspired the author and possible motivations for writing the book.

- **Further reading of sources** mentioned at the back of the book.

- **Bios of authors,** to see if anything they wrote about possibly came from first-hand experience.

- **Historical or cultural context** for books with a particular setting you're not familiar with.

- **Texts that the book was inspired by,** for instance, reading up on Greek mythology for *Circe* by Madeline Miller.

- **Other books by the same author,** for overarching themes or development. Good luck if you're attempting this for, let's say, Margaret Atwood.

- **Looking up specific references** you come across in the book (mentions of other books, foreign words, meaning of names).

- **Watching the film or TV show,** which inevitably will come up in any book club discussion of a book that's been adapted.

As you can see, plenty of extra material to get into, if you choose to do so.

"Because whether we're in the middle of the desert

or in the heart of a city, on the top of a mountain

or on an underground train: having good stories

to keep us company can mean the whole world."

Jen Campbell, *The Bookshop Book*

How to host a digital book club

There are many reasons to take your book club online: if you've got friends in different countries, just can't seem to make your schedule work to meet in person or if you don't have any book lovers in your day-to-day life who you can form a book club with.

A lot of the logistics and tips are the same whether you're online or offline, but there are a few key things to consider to make sure your first online book club runs smoothly.

Before

- **Pick your platform.** You've got loads of different options to choose from to host a video call. While everyone has their personal preference, it's important to pick a platform that has all the functions you might need, and the more people who take part, the more you'll need that extra help.

- **Send an invite.** If you want to encourage as many of your book club members to show up as possible, why not create a fun digital invite? There are lots of websites that will allow you to send beautiful and themed digital invites. And make sure to include a digital calendar event with it too, so that everyone has a reminder in their diary.

- **From personal experience, the cut-off point for a book club on a video call is around ten people.** It's hard to not talk over each other and for everyone to join in with the conversation, so going way over that number wouldn't be recommended.

- **Pick a conversation leader,** just as with a normal book club. This could be the person who picked the book, or someone else who would like to take the role.

- **Get everyone excited!** If you want to add a fun background for the theme of the book, send it around beforehand. Cosy library, Victorian London streets or screenshots from the film adaptation, let your imagination run wild. You can also send around a drink recipe people can make at home. If you're all on social media, why not set a challenge for people to complete, to share the excitement in the lead-up?

During

- **Introductions.** If there are some people in your group who haven't met before, make sure you don't skip the round of introductions. This is also a great opportunity for everyone to get talking and feel more familiar with the group.

- **If you're keen to get the discussion going on time,** as you know your group is likely to stray from the main topic, you can also designate 15 minutes before the call officially starts for everyone to join and catch up.

- **Set the ground rules.** It's worth going over the basics at the beginning of a call, especially if it's your first time getting together online. While many people will have the rules down from work meetings, this might be a new environment for some.

- **Get on the grid view and add your names.** If the service you're using has a grid view, make sure you use it so you can see everyone and keep an eye out so no-one is overlooked.

- **How to not talk over each other.** Muting yourself while you're not speaking ensures that there's not too much background noise. It also has the added benefit that unmuting yourself creates a clear signal that you're getting ready to speak. If you feel like you still can't get through, you can always raise your hand to make it extra clear.

- **If your platform has a chat, this is also a great secondary way to communicate.** Need a bathroom break or just found the quote someone couldn't find while they were talking? Pop it in the chat for everyone to see without having to interrupt someone.

- **Have an end time.** Video call fatigue is a real thing and it's very easy to keep going for a little bit too long. It's often nicer to feel like you could have talked a little more, rather than that you were waiting for it to finally be over.

- **Think about how you can keep the fun going afterwards.** Perhaps you can send out some further reading suggestions (that one person can keep track of during the call) or interesting articles and interviews on the book and topics you discussed.

"I suppose I ought to eat or drink something or other; but the great question is, what?"

Lewis Carroll, *Alice in Wonderland*

Literary-themed snacks and drinks

No book club gathering is complete without food and drinks. Whether you want to create an atmosphere to get even more lost in the setting of the book you'll be discussing or just want to wow your friends with delicious reading-themed snacks, here are some suggestions to get you started. For most of these, you'll be able to adjust them to any dietary needs, opt for alcohol-free versions and go for totally made from scratch or get a helping hand with pre-made items (especially handy if you've still got a few hundred pages to finish before your next book club!).

Food

Cookies for every occasion

There is no shortage of baking in the pages of our favourite classics, and a few of these ideas can definitely apply to a wide range of books. If you want to go general, cookies are very easy to theme. From leaf-shaped cookies, which work for anything autumn or nature themed, to Christmas cookies, and down to the very specific (I've recently become the very proud owner of some adorable Moomin cookie cutters). Yes, there's pretty much a cookie cutter for every theme, or you can get creative making your own shapes. And on a final cookie note, another fun idea is to create simple rectangular biscuits which can be decorated to look like beautiful book covers, although they might require you to set aside most of your day for that activity.

Baked goods from literature

While you're reading your book, keep an eye out for any baked goods that are mentioned. From the apple turnovers in *Little Women* to Dutch *oliebollen* in *The Miniaturist* and even the Queen of Heart's strawberry tarts in *Alice in Wonderland*, there's plenty of inspiration to go around. If you're looking for a feast, why not try your hand at a Regency- or *Anne of Green Gables*-inspired afternoon tea.

What's for dinner?
Is suggesting some Sweeney Todd-themed mini savoury pies a little bit too much? If you're meeting around dinner time, why not go all out and use this as an opportunity to theme your table setting, including place cards with the names of characters from the book you're reading? You can also let yourself be inspired by scenes from *Murder on the Orient Express* by Agatha Christie, a sunny Italian set-up from *Call Me By Your Name*, dumplings and Singapore-style street food from *Crazy Rich Asians*, the feasts featured in *The Great Gatsby* or served in the Great Hall from the *Harry Potter* books. And if that sounds a bit too much, a hearty tomato soup with letter vermicelli and some beautiful old books as table pieces might just do the trick.

Drinks

Cocktails
As with food, there are plenty of options to choose from for your themed drinks. A lot of literary drinks are simply existing cocktails, some of which you can give that literary twist by how you present them. Serve martinis in a thermos flask, reminiscent of drinks by the lake in *The Secret History*, and serve mint juleps in your fanciest glasses on a gold-coloured tray for some Gatsby vibes.

Then there are the imaginary drinks, like the Pan-Galactic Gargle Blaster from *The Hitchhiker's Guide to the Galaxy* (the effect of which is "like having your brains smashed out by a slice of lemon wrapped round a large gold brick"). Any imaginary drinks are a great excuse to let your creativity run wild and raid your pantry for whatever spirits you have, with possibly a hint of food

dye for that "out of this world" look. And for anyone with a sweet tooth, a chocolate cocktail inspired by *Atonement*, with rum, melted chocolate and crushed ice would be a lovely treat. If it's cold out, a Winnie-the-Pooh-themed hot toddy with honey will no doubt be welcomed by your guests.

It's all in the presentation
Transform an ordinary beer or cider into a medieval beverage by serving it in tankards, or turn anything bubbly into a Regency or 20s drink by picking the right elegant glass. You can also recreate Alice's tea party from *Alice in Wonderland* with mismatched tea cups and iced tea cocktails (or, to be honest, any cocktail will do!). Don't forget to play with colours and decorations, like fruit or crushed candy on glass rims.

Non-alcoholic drinks
If some of your guests prefer a non-alcoholic drink, there are quite a few fun ideas to go with too. A raspberry cordial for fans of *Anne of Green Gables*, a hot chocolate from Joanne Harris' *Chocolat*, *His Dark Materials* and many other books, and a wide selection of teas should give you some options. You can also add a touch of magic and whimsy by adding a surprise in your ice cubes, such as edible flowers, fruit or herbs.

Let the setting inspire you
If you're still a bit stuck for ideas and there's nothing that's a specific match, why not let yourself be inspired by the time period or country the book is set in? A quick online search will give you lots of authentic options to choose from, whether they're recipes or items you can pick up at a shop. My favourite tip: name cards for your drink or culinary wonder can make a huge difference, turning bear-shaped cookies into Iorek Byrnison and upgrading a simple cup of tea into a "Mad Hatter's Tea Party Blend".

my
book club
reads

_1_

TITLE:
_____

AUTHOR:
_____

Date started: _____ Date finished: _____

Paperback ☐   Hardback ☐   Ebook ☐   Audiobook ☐

Number of pages: _____

Setting: _____

Book selected by: _____

Book club date: _____ Location: _____

First impressions:
_____
_____
_____
_____
_____
_____
_____
_____
_____

Thoughts after finishing the book:

_____
_____
_____
_____
_____
_____
_____

Themes:

_____
_____
_____
_____
_____
_____
_____

Characters:

_____
_____
_____
_____
_____
_____

Notes and questions:

"The pleasure of all reading is doubled when one lives with another who

Pages to remember:

_____

_____

_____

Final thoughts:

_____

_____

_____

_____

_____

_____

Rating:

_____

Want to reread: Yes ☐   No ☐   Maybe ☐

Further reading:

_____

_____

Favourite quote:

_____

_____

_____

_____

_____

shares the same books." Katherine Mansfield

TITLE:

AUTHOR:

Date started: Date finished:

Paperback ☐   Hardback ☐   Ebook ☐   Audiobook ☐

Number of pages:

Setting:

Book selected by:

Book club date: Location:

First impressions:

Thoughts after finishing the book:

_____
_____
_____
_____
_____
_____
_____

Themes:

_____
_____
_____
_____
_____
_____
_____

Characters:

_____
_____
_____
_____
_____
_____
_____

Notes and questions:

Pages to remember:

_____

_____

Final thoughts:

_____

_____

_____

_____

_____

Rating:

_____

Want to reread: Yes ☐   No ☐   Maybe ☐

Further reading:

_____

_____

Favourite quote:

_____

_____

_____

_____

_____

3

TITLE:
_____

AUTHOR:
_____

Date started: _____ Date finished: _____

Paperback ☐ Hardback ☐ Ebook ☐ Audiobook ☐

Number of pages: _____

Setting: _____

Book selected by: _____

Book club date: _____ Location: _____

First impressions:
_____
_____
_____
_____
_____
_____
_____
_____

Thoughts after finishing the book:

_____
_____
_____
_____
_____
_____
_____

Themes:

_____
_____
_____
_____
_____
_____
_____

Characters:

_____
_____
_____
_____
_____
_____
_____

Notes and questions:

Pages to remember:

Final thoughts:

Rating:

Want to reread: Yes ☐   No ☐   Maybe ☐

Further reading:

Favourite quote:

4

TITLE:
....

AUTHOR:
....

Date started: Date finished:

Paperback ☐   Hardback ☐   Ebook ☐   Audiobook ☐

Number of pages:
....

Setting:
....

Book selected by:
....

Book club date: Location:
....

First impressions:
....
....
....
....
....
....
....
....
....

Thoughts after finishing the book:

_____
_____
_____
_____
_____
_____
_____

Themes:

_____
_____
_____
_____
_____
_____
_____

Characters:

_____
_____
_____
_____
_____
_____
_____

Notes and questions:

"Reading is my favourite occupation, when I have leisure for it

Pages to remember:

_____

_____

_____

Final thoughts:

_____

_____

_____

_____

_____

Rating:

_____

Want to reread: Yes ☐ No ☐ Maybe ☐

Further reading:

_____

_____

Favourite quote:

_____

_____

_____

_____

_____

and books to read." Anne Brontë, *Agnes Grey*

5

TITLE:

AUTHOR:

Date started: Date finished:

Paperback ☐   Hardback ☐   Ebook ☐   Audiobook ☐

Number of pages:

Setting:

Book selected by:

Book club date: Location:

First impressions:

Thoughts after finishing the book:

_____
_____
_____
_____
_____
_____
_____

Themes:

_____
_____
_____
_____
_____
_____

Characters:

_____
_____
_____
_____
_____
_____

Notes and questions:

Pages to remember:

_____

_____

_____

Final thoughts:

_____

_____

_____

_____

_____

_____

Rating:

_____

Want to reread: Yes ☐   No ☐   Maybe ☐

Further reading:

_____

_____

Favourite quote:

_____

_____

_____

_____

_____

_____

6

TITLE:

_____

AUTHOR:

_____

Date started: Date finished:

Paperback ☐ Hardback ☐ Ebook ☐ Audiobook ☐

Number of pages:
_____

Setting:
_____

Book selected by:
_____

Book club date: Location:
_____

First impressions:

_____
_____
_____
_____
_____
_____
_____
_____

Thoughts after finishing the book:

_____
_____
_____
_____
_____
_____
_____
_____

Themes:

_____
_____
_____
_____
_____
_____
_____

Characters:

_____
_____
_____
_____
_____
_____
_____

Notes and questions:

Pages to remember:

Final thoughts:

Rating:

Want to reread: Yes ☐   No ☐   Maybe ☐

Further reading:

Favourite quote:

_7_

TITLE:

AUTHOR:

Date started: Date finished:

Paperback ☐   Hardback ☐   Ebook ☐   Audiobook ☐

Number of pages:

Setting:

Book selected by:

Book club date: Location:

First impressions:

Thoughts after finishing the book:

_____
_____
_____
_____
_____
_____
_____
_____
_____

Themes:

_____
_____
_____
_____
_____
_____
_____
_____

Characters:

_____
_____
_____
_____
_____
_____
_____
_____

Notes and questions:

_____

_____

_____

_____

_____

_____

_____

_____

_____

_____

_____

_____

_____

_____

_____

_____

_____

_____

_____

_____

_____

_____

_____

_____

_____

"That perfect tranquility of life, which is nowhere to be found but in retreat,

Pages to remember:

_____

_____

Final thoughts:

_____

_____

_____

_____

_____

Rating:

_____

Want to reread: Yes ☐   No ☐   Maybe ☐

Further reading:

_____

Favourite quote:

_____

_____

_____

_____

_____

a faithful friend and a good library." Aphra Behn, *The Roundheads*

8

TITLE:

AUTHOR:

Date started: Date finished:

Paperback ☐   Hardback ☐   Ebook ☐   Audiobook ☐

Number of pages:

Setting:

Book selected by:

Book club date: Location:

First impressions:

Thoughts after finishing the book:

_____
_____
_____
_____
_____
_____
_____

Themes:

_____
_____
_____
_____
_____
_____
_____

Characters:

_____
_____
_____
_____
_____
_____

Notes and questions:

Pages to remember:

Final thoughts:

Rating:

Want to reread: Yes ☐　No ☐　Maybe ☐

Further reading:

Favourite quote:

9

TITLE:

AUTHOR:

Date started: Date finished:

Paperback ☐   Hardback ☐   Ebook ☐   Audiobook ☐

Number of pages:

Setting:

Book selected by:

Book club date: Location:

First impressions:

Thoughts after finishing the book:

_____

_____

_____

_____

_____

_____

_____

_____

Themes:

_____

_____

_____

_____

_____

_____

_____

_____

Characters:

_____

_____

_____

_____

_____

_____

_____

_____

Notes and questions:

Pages to remember:

_____

_____

_____

Final thoughts:

_____

_____

_____

_____

_____

Rating:

_____

Want to reread: Yes ☐   No ☐   Maybe ☐

Further reading:

_____

_____

Favourite quote:

_____

_____

_____

_____

_____

TITLE:

_____

AUTHOR:

_____

Date started: _____   Date finished: _____

Paperback ☐   Hardback ☐   Ebook ☐   Audiobook ☐

Number of pages: _____

Setting: _____

Book selected by: _____

Book club date: _____   Location: _____

First impressions:

_____

_____

_____

_____

_____

_____

_____

_____

Thoughts after finishing the book:

_____
_____
_____
_____
_____
_____
_____
_____

Themes:

_____
_____
_____
_____
_____
_____
_____

Characters:

_____
_____
_____
_____
_____
_____
_____

Notes and questions:

"Books may well be the only true magic."

Pages to remember:

Final thoughts:

Rating:

Want to reread: Yes ☐   No ☐   Maybe ☐

Further reading:

Favourite quote:

Alice Hoffman

11

TITLE:

....

AUTHOR:

....

Date started: Date finished:

Paperback ☐   Hardback ☐   Ebook ☐   Audiobook ☐

Number of pages:
....

Setting:
....

Book selected by:
....

Book club date: Location:
....

First impressions:

....

....

....

....

....

....

....

....

Thoughts after finishing the book:

_____
_____
_____
_____
_____
_____
_____
_____

Themes:

_____
_____
_____
_____
_____
_____
_____
_____

Characters:

_____
_____
_____
_____
_____
_____
_____
_____

Notes and questions:

Pages to remember:

Final thoughts:

Rating:

Want to reread: Yes ☐ No ☐ Maybe ☐

Further reading:

Favourite quote:

12

TITLE:
....

AUTHOR:
....

Date started: .... Date finished: ....

Paperback ☐   Hardback ☐   Ebook ☐   Audiobook ☐

Number of pages: ....

Setting: ....

Book selected by: ....

Book club date: .... Location: ....

First impressions: ....

....

....

....

....

....

....

....

....

....

Thoughts after finishing the book:

_____

_____

_____

_____

_____

_____

_____

Themes:

_____

_____

_____

_____

_____

_____

Characters:

_____

_____

_____

_____

_____

_____

Notes and questions:

Pages to remember:

_____

_____

_____

Final thoughts:

_____

_____

_____

_____

_____

_____

Rating:

_____

Want to reread: Yes ☐ No ☐ Maybe ☐

Further reading:

_____

_____

Favourite quote:

_____

_____

_____

_____

_____

13

TITLE:

_____

AUTHOR:

_____

Date started: _____   Date finished: _____

Paperback ☐   Hardback ☐   Ebook ☐   Audiobook ☐

Number of pages: _____
_____

Setting: _____
_____

Book selected by: _____
_____

Book club date: _____   Location: _____
_____

First impressions: _____

_____

_____

_____

_____

_____

_____

_____

_____

_____

Thoughts after finishing the book:

Themes:

Characters:

Notes and questions:

"It is a great thing to start life with a small number of really good books

Pages to remember:

_____

_____

_____

Final thoughts:

_____

_____

_____

_____

_____

Rating:

_____

Want to reread: Yes ☐   No ☐   Maybe ☐

Further reading:

_____

_____

Favourite quote:

_____

_____

_____

_____

_____

_____

which are your very own."   Arthur Conan Doyle

_14_

TITLE:

AUTHOR:

Date started: Date finished:

Paperback ☐   Hardback ☐   Ebook ☐   Audiobook ☐

Number of pages:

Setting:

Book selected by:

Book club date: Location:

First impressions:

Thoughts after finishing the book:

Themes:

Characters:

Notes and questions:

Pages to remember:

_____

_____

_____

Final thoughts:

_____

_____

_____

_____

_____

_____

Rating:

_____

Want to reread: Yes ☐   No ☐   Maybe ☐

Further reading:

_____

_____

Favourite quote:

_____

_____

_____

_____

_____

_____

15

TITLE:
_____

AUTHOR:
_____

Date started: _____ Date finished: _____

Paperback ☐   Hardback ☐   Ebook ☐   Audiobook ☐

Number of pages: _____

Setting: _____

Book selected by: _____

Book club date: _____   Location: _____

First impressions:
_____
_____
_____
_____
_____
_____
_____

Thoughts after finishing the book:

_____
_____
_____
_____
_____
_____
_____
_____

Themes:

_____
_____
_____
_____
_____
_____
_____
_____

Characters:

_____
_____
_____
_____
_____
_____
_____
_____

Notes and questions:

Pages to remember:

Final thoughts:

Rating:

Want to reread: Yes ☐   No ☐   Maybe ☐

Further reading:

Favourite quote:

16

TITLE:
....

AUTHOR:
....

Date started: .... Date finished: ....

Paperback ☐   Hardback ☐   Ebook ☐   Audiobook ☐

Number of pages: ....
....

Setting: ....
....

Book selected by: ....
....

Book club date: .... Location: ....
....

First impressions: ....

....

....

....

....

....

....

....

....

Thoughts after finishing the book:

_____
_____
_____
_____
_____
_____
_____
_____

Themes:

_____
_____
_____
_____
_____
_____
_____
_____

Characters:

_____
_____
_____
_____
_____
_____
_____
_____

Notes and questions:

"To learn to read is to light a fire; every syllable that is spelled out is a spark."

Pages to remember:

_____

_____

_____

Final thoughts:

_____

_____

_____

_____

_____

Rating:

_____

Want to reread: Yes ☐ No ☐ Maybe ☐

Further reading:

_____

_____

Favourite quote:

_____

_____

_____

_____

_____

Victor Hugo, *Les Misérables*

17

TITLE:

AUTHOR:

Date started: Date finished:

Paperback ☐   Hardback ☐   Ebook ☐   Audiobook ☐

Number of pages:

Setting:

Book selected by:

Book club date: Location:

First impressions:

Thoughts after finishing the book:

_____
_____
_____
_____
_____
_____
_____
_____

Themes:

_____
_____
_____
_____
_____
_____
_____

Characters:

_____
_____
_____
_____
_____
_____
_____

Notes and questions:

Pages to remember:

Final thoughts:

Rating:

Want to reread: Yes ☐   No ☐   Maybe ☐

Further reading:

Favourite quote:

18

TITLE:

AUTHOR:

Date started: Date finished:

Paperback ☐   Hardback ☐   Ebook ☐   Audiobook ☐

Number of pages:

Setting:

Book selected by:

Book club date: Location:

First impressions:

Thoughts after finishing the book:

_____

_____

_____

_____

_____

_____

_____

Themes:

_____

_____

_____

_____

_____

_____

Characters:

_____

_____

_____

_____

_____

_____

Notes and questions:

Pages to remember:

Final thoughts:

Rating:

Want to reread: Yes ☐   No ☐   Maybe ☐

Further reading:

Favourite quote:

19

TITLE:
....

AUTHOR:
....

Date started: Date finished:

Paperback ☐   Hardback ☐   Ebook ☐   Audiobook ☐

Number of pages:
....

Setting:
....

Book selected by:
....

Book club date: Location:
....

First impressions:
....
....
....
....
....
....
....
....
....
....

Thoughts after finishing the book:

_____
_____
_____
_____
_____
_____
_____
_____

Themes:

_____
_____
_____
_____
_____
_____

Characters:

_____
_____
_____
_____
_____
_____

Notes and questions:

"Books are the mirrors of the soul."

Pages to remember:

Final thoughts:

Rating:

Want to reread: Yes ☐   No ☐   Maybe ☐

Further reading:

Favourite quote:

Virginia Woolf, *Between the Acts*

20

TITLE:
....

AUTHOR:
....

Date started: Date finished:

Paperback ☐   Hardback ☐   Ebook ☐   Audiobook ☐

Number of pages:
....

Setting:
....

Book selected by:
....

Book club date: Location:
....

First impressions:
....
....
....
....
....
....
....
....
....
....

Thoughts after finishing the book:

_____
_____
_____
_____
_____
_____
_____
_____

Themes:

_____
_____
_____
_____
_____
_____
_____
_____

Characters:

_____
_____
_____
_____
_____
_____
_____

Notes and questions:

Pages to remember:

_____

_____

Final thoughts:

_____

_____

_____

_____

_____

_____

Rating:

_____

Want to reread. Yes ☐   No ☐   Maybe ☐

Further reading:

_____

_____

Favourite quote:

_____

_____

_____

_____

_____

_____

TITLE:
_____

AUTHOR:
_____

Date started: Date finished:

Paperback ☐   Hardback ☐   Ebook ☐   Audiobook ☐

Number of pages:
_____

Setting:
_____

Book selected by:
_____

Book club date: Location:
_____

First impressions:
_____
_____
_____
_____
_____
_____
_____
_____

Thoughts after finishing the book:

_____

_____

_____

_____

_____

_____

_____

Themes:

_____

_____

_____

_____

_____

_____

_____

Characters:

_____

_____

_____

_____

_____

_____

_____

Notes and questions:

Pages to remember:

Final thoughts:

Rating:

Want to reread: Yes ☐   No ☐   Maybe ☐

Further reading:

Favourite quote:

TITLE:

_____

AUTHOR:

_____

Date started: Date finished:

Paperback ☐   Hardback ☐   Ebook ☐   Audiobook ☐

Number of pages:
_____

Setting:
_____

Book selected by:
_____

Book club date: Location:
_____

First impressions:
_____
_____
_____
_____
_____
_____
_____
_____

Thoughts after finishing the book:

_____

_____

_____

_____

_____

_____

_____

Themes:

_____

_____

_____

_____

_____

_____

Characters:

_____

_____

_____

_____

_____

_____

Notes and questions:

"A book must be the axe for the frozen sea within us."

Pages to remember:

_____

_____

_____

Final thoughts:

_____

_____

_____

_____

_____

Rating:

_____

Want to reread: Yes ☐   No ☐   Maybe ☐

Further reading:

_____

_____

Favourite quote:

_____

_____

_____

_____

_____

Franz Kafka

23

TITLE:
....

AUTHOR:
....

Date started: Date finished:

Paperback ☐   Hardback ☐   Ebook ☐   Audiobook ☐

Number of pages:
....

Setting:
....

Book selected by:
....

Book club date: Location:
....

First impressions:
....
....
....
....
....
....
....
....
....
....

Thoughts after finishing the book:

_____
_____
_____
_____
_____
_____
_____

Themes:

_____
_____
_____
_____
_____
_____
_____

Characters:

_____
_____
_____
_____
_____
_____
_____

Notes and questions:

Pages to remember:

Final thoughts:

Rating:

Want to reread: Yes ☐   No ☐   Maybe ☐

Further reading:

Favourite quote:

TITLE:
....

AUTHOR:
....

Date started: Date finished:

Paperback ☐   Hardback ☐   Ebook ☐   Audiobook ☐

Number of pages:
....

Setting:
....

Book selected by:
....

Book club date: Location:
....

First impressions:
....
....
....
....
....
....
....
....
....

Thoughts after finishing the book:

_____
_____
_____
_____
_____
_____
_____
_____

Themes:

_____
_____
_____
_____
_____
_____
_____

Characters:

_____
_____
_____
_____
_____
_____

Notes and questions:

Pages to remember:

Final thoughts:

Rating:

Want to reread: Yes ☐   No ☐   Maybe ☐

Further reading:

Favourite quote:

25

TITLE:

AUTHOR:

Date started: Date finished:

Paperback ☐   Hardback ☐   Ebook ☐   Audiobook ☐

Number of pages:

Setting:

Book selected by:

Book club date: Location:

First impressions:

Thoughts after finishing the book:

_____
_____
_____
_____
_____
_____
_____

Themes:

_____
_____
_____
_____
_____
_____

Characters:

_____
_____
_____
_____
_____
_____

Notes and questions:

"Read the best books first, or you may not have a chance to read them at all."

Pages to remember:

_____

_____

_____

Final thoughts:

_____

_____

_____

_____

_____

_____

Rating:

_____

Want to reread: Yes ☐   No ☐   Maybe ☐

Further reading:

_____

_____

Favourite quote:

_____

_____

_____

_____

_____

Henry David Thoreau, *A Week on the Concord and Merrimack Rivers*

26

TITLE:

....

AUTHOR:

....

Date started: Date finished:

Paperback ☐   Hardback ☐   Ebook ☐   Audiobook ☐

Number of pages:

....

Setting:

....

Book selected by:

....

Book club date: Location:

....

First impressions:

....

....

....

....

....

....

....

....

....

Thoughts after finishing the book:

_____

_____

_____

_____

_____

_____

_____

Themes:

_____

_____

_____

_____

_____

_____

Characters:

_____

_____

_____

_____

_____

_____

Notes and questions:

Pages to remember:

Final thoughts:

Rating:

Want to reread: Yes ☐ No ☐ Maybe ☐

Further reading:

Favourite quote:

27

TITLE:

_____

AUTHOR:

_____

Date started: _____ Date finished: _____

Paperback ☐   Hardback ☐   Ebook ☐   Audiobook ☐

Number of pages: _____

Setting: _____

Book selected by: _____

Book club date: _____ Location: _____

First impressions:

_____

_____

_____

_____

_____

_____

_____

_____

Thoughts after finishing the book:

_____
_____
_____
_____
_____
_____
_____

Themes:

_____
_____
_____
_____
_____
_____
_____

Characters:

_____
_____
_____
_____
_____
_____
_____

Notes and questions:

Pages to remember:

_____

_____

_____

Final thoughts:

_____

_____

_____

_____

_____

_____

Rating:

_____

Want to reread: Yes ☐   No ☐   Maybe ☐

Further reading:

_____

_____

Favourite quote:

_____

_____

_____

_____

_____

_____

28

TITLE:

AUTHOR:

Date started: Date finished:

Paperback ☐   Hardback ☐   Ebook ☐   Audiobook ☐

Number of pages:

Setting:

Book selected by:

Book club date: Location:

First impressions:

Thoughts after finishing the book:

_____
_____
_____
_____
_____
_____
_____

Themes:

_____
_____
_____
_____
_____
_____

Characters:

_____
_____
_____
_____
_____
_____

Notes and questions:

"Literature is the most agreeable way of ignoring life."

Pages to remember:

_____

_____

_____

Final thoughts:

_____

_____

_____

_____

_____

_____

Rating:

_____

Want to reread: Yes ☐   No ☐   Maybe ☐

Further reading:

_____

_____

Favourite quote:

_____

_____

_____

_____

_____

Fernando Pessoa, *The Book of Disquiet*

TITLE:

AUTHOR:

Date started: Date finished:

Paperback ☐   Hardback ☐   Ebook ☐   Audiobook ☐

Number of pages:

Setting:

Book selected by:

Book club date: Location:

First impressions:

Thoughts after finishing the book:

_____
_____
_____
_____
_____
_____
_____

Themes:

_____
_____
_____
_____
_____
_____
_____

Characters:

_____
_____
_____
_____
_____
_____
_____

Notes and questions:

Pages to remember:

_____

_____

_____

Final thoughts:

_____

_____

_____

_____

_____

_____

Rating:

_____

Want to reread: Yes ☐   No ☐   Maybe ☐

Further reading:

_____

_____

Favourite quote:

_____

_____

_____

_____

_____

_____

30

TITLE:

AUTHOR:

Date started: Date finished:

Paperback ☐   Hardback ☐   Ebook ☐   Audiobook ☐

Number of pages:

Setting:

Book selected by:

Book club date: Location:

First impressions:

Thoughts after finishing the book:

_____

_____

_____

_____

_____

_____

_____

Themes:

_____

_____

_____

_____

_____

_____

_____

Characters:

_____

_____

_____

_____

_____

_____

_____

Notes and questions:

Pages to remember:

_____
_____
_____

Final thoughts:

_____
_____
_____
_____
_____
_____

Rating:

_____

Want to reread: Yes ☐   No ☐   Maybe ☐

Further reading:

_____
_____

Favourite quote:

_____
_____
_____
_____
_____
_____

TITLE:

....

AUTHOR:

....

Date started: Date finished:

Paperback ☐   Hardback ☐   Ebook ☐   Audiobook ☐

Number of pages:
....

Setting:
....

Book selected by:
....

Book club date: Location:
....

First impressions:

....

....

....

....

....

....

....

....

Thoughts after finishing the book:

_____

_____

_____

_____

_____

_____

_____

_____

Themes:

_____

_____

_____

_____

_____

_____

_____

Characters:

_____

_____

_____

_____

_____

_____

_____

Notes and questions:

"No entertainment is so cheap as reading, nor any pleasure so lasting."

Pages to remember:

Final thoughts:

Rating:

Want to reread: Yes ☐   No ☐   Maybe ☐

Further reading:

Favourite quote:

Lady Mary Wortley Montagu

32

TITLE:

_____

AUTHOR:

_____

Date started: Date finished:

Paperback ☐   Hardback ☐   Ebook ☐   Audiobook ☐

Number of pages:
_____

Setting:
_____

Book selected by:
_____

Book club date: Location:
_____

First impressions:

_____

_____

_____

_____

_____

_____

_____

_____

_____

Thoughts after finishing the book:

_____

_____

_____

_____

_____

_____

_____

Themes:

_____

_____

_____

_____

_____

_____

_____

Characters:

_____

_____

_____

_____

_____

_____

_____

Notes and questions:

Pages to remember:

_____

_____

_____

Final thoughts:

_____

_____

_____

_____

_____

Rating:

_____

Want to reread: Yes ☐   No ☐   Maybe ☐

Further reading:

_____

_____

Favourite quote:

_____

_____

_____

_____

_____

TITLE:

_____

AUTHOR:

_____

Date started: Date finished:

Paperback ☐   Hardback ☐   Ebook ☐   Audiobook ☐

Number of pages:

_____

Setting:

_____

Book selected by:

_____

Book club date: Location:

_____

First impressions:

_____

_____

_____

_____

_____

_____

_____

_____

_____

Thoughts after finishing the book:

Themes:

Characters:

Notes and questions:

Pages to remember:

_____

_____

_____

Final thoughts:

_____

_____

_____

_____

_____

_____

Rating:

_____

Want to reread: Yes ☐   No ☐   Maybe ☐

Further reading:

_____

_____

Favourite quote:

_____

_____

_____

_____

_____

_____

34

TITLE:

AUTHOR:

Date started: Date finished:

Paperback ☐   Hardback ☐   Ebook ☐   Audiobook ☐

Number of pages:

Setting:

Book selected by:

Book club date: Location:

First impressions:

Thoughts after finishing the book:

_____

_____

_____

_____

_____

_____

_____

_____

Themes:

_____

_____

_____

_____

_____

_____

_____

Characters:

_____

_____

_____

_____

_____

_____

_____

Notes and questions:

"There is no Frigate like a Book. To take us Lands away."

Pages to remember:

Final thoughts:

Rating:

Want to reread: Yes ☐   No ☐   Maybe ☐

Further reading:

Favourite quote:

Emily Dickinson, "There is No Frigate like a Book"

35

TITLE:

AUTHOR:

Date started: Date finished:

Paperback ☐   Hardback ☐   Ebook ☐   Audiobook ☐

Number of pages:

Setting:

Book selected by:

Book club date: Location:

First impressions:

Thoughts after finishing the book:

_____

_____

_____

_____

_____

_____

_____

Themes:

_____

_____

_____

_____

_____

_____

Characters:

_____

_____

_____

_____

_____

_____

Notes and questions:

Pages to remember:

_____

_____

Final thoughts:

_____

_____

_____

_____

_____

Rating:

_____

Want to reread: Yes ☐   No ☐   Maybe ☐

Further reading:

_____

_____

Favourite quote:

_____

_____

_____

_____

_____

36

TITLE:
....

AUTHOR:
....

Date started: Date finished:

Paperback ☐   Hardback ☐   Ebook ☐   Audiobook ☐

Number of pages:
....

Setting:
....

Book selected by:
....

Book club date: Location:
....

First impressions:
....
....
....
....
....
....
....
....
....

Thoughts after finishing the book:

_____
_____
_____
_____
_____
_____
_____

Themes:

_____
_____
_____
_____
_____
_____
_____

Characters:

_____
_____
_____
_____
_____
_____
_____

Notes and questions:

Pages to remember:

_____

_____

_____

Final thoughts:

_____

_____

_____

_____

_____

Rating:

_____

Want to reread: Yes ☐   No ☐   Maybe ☐

Further reading:

_____

_____

Favourite quote:

_____

_____

_____

_____

_____

37

TITLE:
_____

AUTHOR:
_____

Date started: Date finished:

Paperback ☐   Hardback ☐   Ebook ☐   Audiobook ☐

Number of pages:
_____

Setting:
_____

Book selected by:
_____

Book club date: Location:
_____

First impressions:
_____
_____
_____
_____
_____
_____
_____
_____
_____

Thoughts after finishing the book:

_____
_____
_____
_____
_____
_____
_____

Themes:

_____
_____
_____
_____
_____
_____
_____

Characters:

_____
_____
_____
_____
_____
_____

Notes and questions:

"Come, and take choice of all my library, And so beguile thy sorrow."

Pages to remember:

_____

_____

_____

Final thoughts:

_____

_____

_____

_____

_____

Rating:

_____

Want to reread: Yes ☐   No ☐   Maybe ☐

Further reading:

_____

_____

Favourite quote:

_____

_____

_____

_____

_____

William Shakespeare, *Titus Andronicus, Act 4, Scene 1*

38

TITLE:

AUTHOR:

Date started: Date finished:

Paperback ☐   Hardback ☐   Ebook ☐   Audiobook ☐

Number of pages:

Setting:

Book selected by:

Book club date: Location:

First impressions:

Thoughts after finishing the book:

_____
_____
_____
_____
_____
_____
_____
_____

Themes:

_____
_____
_____
_____
_____
_____
_____

Characters:

_____
_____
_____
_____
_____
_____
_____

Notes and questions:

Pages to remember:

_____
_____

Final thoughts:

_____
_____
_____
_____
_____
_____

Rating:

_____

Want to reread: Yes ☐   No ☐   Maybe ☐

Further reading:

_____
_____

Favourite quote:

_____
_____
_____
_____
_____

TITLE:

....

AUTHOR:

....

Date started: Date finished:

Paperback ☐   Hardback ☐   Ebook ☐   Audiobook ☐

Number of pages:

....

Setting:

....

Book selected by:

....

Book club date: Location:

....

First impressions:

....

....

....

....

....

....

....

....

....

Thoughts after finishing the book:

_____

_____

_____

_____

_____

_____

_____

_____

Themes:

_____

_____

_____

_____

_____

_____

_____

Characters:

_____

_____

_____

_____

_____

_____

Notes and questions:

Pages to remember:

_____

_____

_____

Final thoughts:

_____

_____

_____

_____

_____

Rating:

_____

Want to reread: Yes ☐   No ☐   Maybe ☐

Further reading:

_____

_____

Favourite quote:

_____

_____

_____

_____

_____

40

TITLE:
....

AUTHOR:
....

Date started: .... Date finished: ....

Paperback ☐   Hardback ☐   Ebook ☐   Audiobook ☐

Number of pages: ....

Setting: ....

Book selected by: ....

Book club date: .... Location: ....

First impressions:
....
....
....
....
....
....
....
....
....
....

Thoughts after finishing the book:

_____
_____
_____
_____
_____
_____
_____

Themes:

_____
_____
_____
_____
_____
_____
_____

Characters:

_____
_____
_____
_____
_____
_____
_____

Notes and questions:

"Reading brings us unknown friends."

Pages to remember:

_____
_____
_____

Final thoughts:

_____
_____
_____
_____
_____
_____

Rating:

_____

Want to reread: Yes ☐   No ☐   Maybe ☐

Further reading:

_____
_____

Favourite quote:

_____
_____
_____
_____
_____

Honoré de Balzac

41

TITLE:
_____

AUTHOR:
_____

Date started: _____ Date finished: _____

Paperback ☐   Hardback ☐   Ebook ☐   Audiobook ☐

Number of pages: _____

Setting: _____

Book selected by: _____

Book club date: _____ Location: _____

First impressions:
_____
_____
_____
_____
_____
_____
_____
_____
_____

Thoughts after finishing the book:

_____

_____

_____

_____

_____

_____

_____

_____

Themes:

_____

_____

_____

_____

_____

_____

_____

Characters:

_____

_____

_____

_____

_____

_____

Notes and questions:

Pages to remember:

_____

_____

_____

Final thoughts:

_____

_____

_____

_____

_____

Rating:

_____

Want to reread: Yes ☐   No ☐   Maybe ☐

Further reading:

_____

_____

Favourite quote:

_____

_____

_____

_____

_____

_42_

TITLE:

_____

AUTHOR:

_____

Date started: Date finished:

Paperback ☐   Hardback ☐   Ebook ☐   Audiobook ☐

Number of pages:
_____

Setting:
_____

Book selected by:
_____

Book club date: Location:
_____

First impressions:

_____

_____

_____

_____

_____

_____

_____

_____

_____

_____

Thoughts after finishing the book:

_____
_____
_____
_____
_____
_____
_____

Themes:

_____
_____
_____
_____
_____
_____
_____

Characters:

_____
_____
_____
_____
_____
_____
_____

Notes and questions:

Pages to remember:

_____

_____

_____

Final thoughts:

_____

_____

_____

_____

_____

Rating:

_____

Want to reread: Yes ☐   No ☐   Maybe ☐

Further reading:

_____

_____

Favourite quote:

_____

_____

_____

_____

_____

43

TITLE:

_____

AUTHOR:

_____

Date started: _____ Date finished: _____

Paperback ☐ Hardback ☐ Ebook ☐ Audiobook ☐

Number of pages: _____

Setting: _____

Book selected by: _____

Book club date: _____ Location: _____

First impressions:

_____

_____

_____

_____

_____

_____

_____

_____

_____

Thoughts after finishing the book:

_____

_____

_____

_____

_____

_____

_____

Themes:

_____

_____

_____

_____

_____

_____

_____

Characters:

_____

_____

_____

_____

_____

_____

_____

Notes and questions:

"You don't have to burn books to destroy a culture.

Pages to remember:

Final thoughts:

Rating:

Want to reread: Yes ☐ No ☐ Maybe ☐

Further reading:

Favourite quote:

Just get people to stop reading them." Ray Bradbury, *Fahrenheit 451*

44

TITLE:

....

AUTHOR:

....

Date started: Date finished:

Paperback ☐ Hardback ☐ Ebook ☐ Audiobook ☐

Number of pages:

....

Setting:

....

Book selected by:

....

Book club date: Location:

....

First impressions:

....

....

....

....

....

....

....

....

....

Thoughts after finishing the book:

_____
_____
_____
_____
_____
_____
_____
_____

Themes:

_____
_____
_____
_____
_____
_____
_____

Characters:

_____
_____
_____
_____
_____
_____
_____

Notes and questions:

Pages to remember:

Final thoughts:

Rating:

Want to reread: Yes ☐   No ☐   Maybe ☐

Further reading:

Favourite quote:

45

TITLE:
_____

AUTHOR:
_____

Date started: _____ Date finished: _____

Paperback ☐ Hardback ☐ Ebook ☐ Audiobook ☐

Number of pages: _____

Setting: _____

Book selected by: _____

Book club date: _____ Location: _____

First impressions:
_____
_____
_____
_____
_____
_____
_____
_____
_____

Thoughts after finishing the book:

_____
_____
_____
_____
_____
_____
_____

Themes:

_____
_____
_____
_____
_____
_____

Characters:

_____
_____
_____
_____
_____
_____

Notes and questions:

Pages to remember:

Final thoughts:

Rating:

Want to reread: Yes ☐   No ☐   Maybe ☐

Further reading:

Favourite quote:

TITLE:

AUTHOR:

Date started: Date finished:

Paperback ☐   Hardback ☐   Ebook ☐   Audiobook ☐

Number of pages:

Setting:

Book selected by:

Book club date: Location:

First impressions:

Thoughts after finishing the book:

_____
_____
_____
_____
_____
_____
_____

Themes:

_____
_____
_____
_____
_____
_____

Characters:

_____
_____
_____
_____
_____
_____

Notes and questions:

"People say that life is the thing, but I prefer reading."

Pages to remember:

_____

_____

Final thoughts:

_____

_____

_____

_____

_____

Rating:

_____

Want to reread: Yes ☐   No ☐   Maybe ☐

Further reading:

_____

_____

Favourite quote:

_____

_____

_____

_____

_____

_____

Logan Pearsall Smith

TITLE:

AUTHOR:

Date started: Date finished:

Paperback ☐   Hardback ☐   Ebook ☐   Audiobook ☐

Number of pages:

Setting:

Book selected by:

Book club date: Location:

First impressions:

Thoughts after finishing the book:

_____
_____
_____
_____
_____
_____
_____

Themes:

_____
_____
_____
_____
_____
_____
_____

Characters:

_____
_____
_____
_____
_____
_____
_____

Notes and questions:

Pages to remember:

Final thoughts:

Rating:

Want to reread: Yes ☐   No ☐   Maybe ☐

Further reading:

Favourite quote:

TITLE:

_____

AUTHOR:

_____

Date started: _____ Date finished: _____

Paperback ☐ Hardback ☐ Ebook ☐ Audiobook ☐

Number of pages: _____

Setting: _____

Book selected by: _____

Book club date: _____ Location: _____

First impressions:

_____

_____

_____

_____

_____

_____

_____

_____

Thoughts after finishing the book:

_____

_____

_____

_____

_____

_____

_____

Themes:

_____

_____

_____

_____

_____

_____

Characters:

_____

_____

_____

_____

_____

_____

Notes and questions:

Pages to remember:

Final thoughts:

Rating:

Want to reread: Yes ☐   No ☐   Maybe ☐

Further reading:

Favourite quote:

49

TITLE:

AUTHOR:

Date started: Date finished:

Paperback ☐   Hardback ☐   Ebook ☐   Audiobook ☐

Number of pages:

Setting:

Book selected by:

Book club date: Location:

First impressions:

Thoughts after finishing the book:

_____

_____

_____

_____

_____

_____

_____

Themes:

_____

_____

_____

_____

_____

_____

_____

Characters:

_____

_____

_____

_____

_____

_____

Notes and questions:

"The person, be it gentleman or lady, who has not pleasure in a good novel,

Pages to remember:

_____

_____

_____

Final thoughts:

_____

_____

_____

_____

_____

Rating:

_____

Want to reread: Yes ☐   No ☐   Maybe ☐

Further reading:

_____

_____

Favourite quote:

_____

_____

_____

_____

_____

must be intolerably stupid."   Jane Austen, *Northanger Abbey*

50

TITLE:

AUTHOR:

Date started: Date finished:

Paperback ☐   Hardback ☐   Ebook ☐   Audiobook ☐

Number of pages:

Setting:

Book selected by:

Book club date: Location:

First impressions:

Thoughts after finishing the book:

_____

_____

_____

_____

_____

_____

_____

Themes:

_____

_____

_____

_____

_____

_____

Characters:

_____

_____

_____

_____

_____

_____

Notes and questions:

Pages to remember:

Final thoughts:

Rating:

Want to reread: Yes ☐　No ☐　Maybe ☐

Further reading:

Favourite quote:

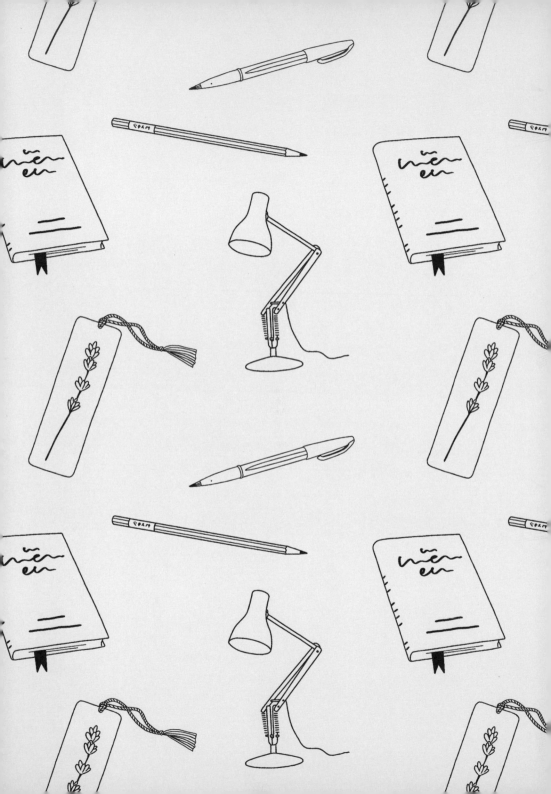

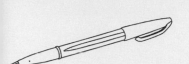

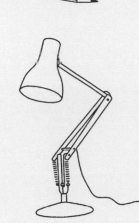
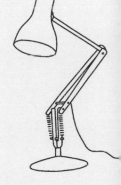

reading
lists and
logs

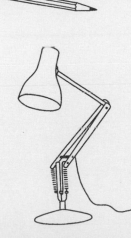

Longbourn
Jo Baker
A new perspective on Jane Austen's
Pride and Prejudice, as told by the servants
at Longbourn.

The Song of Achilles
Madeline Miller
The heartbreaking story of Patroclus and
Achilles, from their meeting as young
boys to the tragic Trojan War.

The Deathless Girls
Kiran Millwood Hargrave
The origin tale of Dracula's brides, which
centres on the strong bond between twin
sisters Kizzy and Lil, who are captured
by the cruel Boyar Valcar.

Wide Sargasso Sea
Jean Rhys
The mesmerizing story of Antoinette
Cosway shines a different light on the
madwoman in the attic in Charlotte
Brontë's *Jane Eyre*.

The Hours
Michael Cunningham
Visit 1920s London, 1940s Los Angeles
and 1990s New York and get lost in three
stories that are all intertwined with
Virginia Woolf's *Mrs Dalloway*.

The Vegetarian
Han Kang
When Yeong-hye decides to stop eating
meat after a nightmare, she slowly
becomes distanced from society. An
intriguing three-part book with allusions
to the story of Daphne and Apollo.

Home Fire
Kamila Shamsie
A retelling of the Greek myth of Antigone,
this book centres around the themes
of family, loyalty and radicalization.

The Other Bennet Sister
Janice Hadlow
What would happen if Mary Bennet
took a different path than what was laid
out for her in *Pride and Prejudice*?

The Bear and the Nightingale
Katherine Arden
Inspired by Russian folklore, this is
magical tale of a rebellious girl in rural
Russia, who is the only one in her town
who can talk to the household spirits and
is threatened by an ancient force.

Everything Under
Daisy Johnson
When the past comes rushing back with
a single phone call from her missing
mother, Gretel has to face her old fears.
A tale inspired by Greek mythology.

Turtles All the Way Down
John Green
The touching story of Aza Holmes, featuring a fugitive billionaire, *Star Wars* fanfiction and a tuatara, with the ups and downs of friendship and mental health at the heart of it.

Oranges Are Not the Only Fruit
Jeanette Winterson
Join a young girl as she comes to terms with her sexuality while living in a strict religious environment. Funny, heartbreaking and totally unique.

Black Flamingo
Dean Atta
A colourful and energetic verse novel featuring a mixed-race gay teen who is finding his place in the world.

Go Tell It on the Mountain
James Baldwin
A 14-year-old boy's journey of discovering himself and his relationship with his family, church and the world around him, set in 1930s Harlem.

The Virgin Suicides
Jeffrey Eugenides
Twenty years on, a group of boys share their memories of the mysterious Lux sisters in this poetic, dream-like and sometimes shocking novel.

The Miseducation of Cameron Post
Emily M Danforth
Cameron Post's vivid account of the loss of her parents, her first kiss with a girl during the blistering Montana summer and her forced move to a Christian conversion-therapy camp.

Jane Eyre
Charlotte Brontë
A classic following an orphaned girl as she tries to find her place in the world and starts working as a governess at Thornfield Hall for the mysterious and brooding Mr Rochester.

Loveless
Alice Oseman
Georgia has never had a crush on anyone and isn't sure what that means. Then she's thrown into a brand-new world of university, roommates and friendship upheaval.

The Bluest Eye
Toni Morrison
Toni Morrison's first, unforgettable novel, set in 1940s Ohio, tells the tragic story of a young black girl called Pecola Breedlove, during the years after the Great Depression.

Speak
Laurie Halse Anderson
A classic of the genre, following funny, observant and friendless freshman Melinda, who's been alienated for calling the police during a summer party.

Educated
Tara Westover
A story so unbelievable it reads like fiction, chronicling the life of a young girl growing up with her family in rural Idaho, as they prepare for the end of the world.

Fun Home
Alison Bechdel
A memoir in graphic novel form, focusing on sexuality, self-discovery and dysfunctional family life.

Hunger
Roxane Gay
A difficult and honest text, all about Roxane's body, from child to adult, and her personal and public experience of being overweight.

Wild
Cheryl Strayed
"A journey from lost to found", following 26-year-old Cheryl as she hikes along the Pacific Crest Trail, without any previous experience, at the lowest point in her life.

Between the World and Me
Ta-Nehisi Coates
Written in the form of a letter to his son, Ta-Nehisi tackles questions around race in America.

Becoming
Michelle Obama
From childhood to the White House, follow Michelle Obama's family life, career, relationships and the experiences that shaped her.

This Is Going to Hurt
Adam Kay
The secret, hilarious and poignant diaries of a junior doctor, as told through short anecdotes that will stay with you long after you close the book.

Brit(ish)
Afua Hirsch
Why do people keep asking you where you're from? An exploration of race and identity in Britain today, part historical analysis and part memoir.

The Gender Games
Juno Dawson
A funny and honest social commentary on gender and trans issues in society, also featuring insights from a range of gender, feminist and trans activists.

When Breath Becomes Air
Paul Kalanithi
The heart-rending memoir of a neurosurgeon who is diagnosed with stage IV lung cancer, and his journey from doctor to patient.

The Fifth Season
N K Jemisin
This Hugo Award-winning first book
in *The Broken Earth* trilogy is set during
the start of a catastrophic climate change
event. Both heartbreaking and magical,
it uses exceptional world-building to
explore nature and race.

The Martian
Andy Weir
When astronaut Mark Watney is left for
dead on Mars after a dust storm, he has to
use all his engineering skills, perseverance
and sense of humour to stay alive by
himself. A high-tension and equally
funny and compelling read.

The Long Way to a Small, Angry Planet
Becky Chambers
Join a diverse crew of characters
on a space adventure on the *Wayfarer*.
A must-read for fans of space operas
and the TV show *Firefly*.

The Loneliest Girl in the Universe
Lauren James
Meet Romy, a teenage girl who is the
last surviving crew member of a space
mission. Everything changes when she
gets a message that the situation on Earth
has changed dramatically and a ship is
coming to find her.

Solaris
Stanislaw Lem
A Polish classic set in a space station on
the planet Solaris, where a newly arrived
astronaut encounters more and more
strange discoveries.

The Left Hand of Darkness
Ursula K Le Guin
This groundbreaking sci-fi novel,
covering psychology, society, gender and
friendship, follows Genly Ai, a human
who is sent to convince the citizens of the
planet Gethen to join the confederation
of planets.

On a Sunbeam
Tillie Walden
A thoughtful and beautifully illustrated
graphic novel about Mia, who joins a
crew that's restoring ruins in space, but
can't forget the girl she fell in love with
at school.

Cloud Atlas
David Mitchell
Get ready to jump through time and
space, from character to character,
in this mind-bending novel.

Binti
Nnedi Okorafor
Binti is the first of the Himba people
to get offered a place at a prestigious
university on a faraway planet and starts
a tumultuous journey to get there.

All Systems Red
Martha Wells
A team of scientists embarks on a perilous
expedition to an alien planet. They're
accompanied by an android that, having
hacked its own hardware, has begun to
develop self-awareness and refers to itself
as "Murderbot".

NW
Zadie Smith
Follow four Londoners as they try to figure out adult life and everything that comes with it, from class to self-discovery and social pressures.

The Lonely Londoners
Sam Selvon
A classic novel about immigrant life in London in the 1950s.

Convenience Store Woman
Sayaka Murata
A quirky short book about 36-year-old Keiko, who lives in Tokyo and has been working in the same supermarket for the past 18 years.

Fingersmith
Sarah Waters
The life of Sue Trinder, an orphan in Victorian London, changes when she's asked to become the maid to a naive gentlewoman, as part of a scheme to steal her inheritance.

Faces in the Crowd
Valeria Luiselli
You'll travel from Mexico City to Harlem, to Philadelphia and back to New York as you move from character to character, all within intersecting stories.

Brooklyn
Colm Tóibín
In this novel, set between Brooklyn and Ireland in the early 1950s, the young Eilis makes her way across the ocean to find a new life, and has to decide where her future lies.

Tokyo Ueno Station
Yu Miri
Set against the history of both the 1964 Tokyo Olympics and the anticipation of the 2020 Olympics, this novel introduces you to the ghost of a labourer who haunts the park near Ueno Station.

Mrs Dalloway
Virginia Woolf
Virginia Woolf's most famous novel follows a woman's movements and inner thoughts for a day as she walks through London and prepares for a dinner party.

Reading Lolita in Tehran
Azar Nafisi
A memoir about a group of women who meet in secret to discuss forbidden books, such as *The Great Gatsby* and *Pride and Prejudice*, while also sharing their own stories, together with their teacher.

The Amazing Adventures of Kavalier and Clay
Michael Chabon
Set in Prague and New York (and the Arctic) in the 1930s, join Josef Kavalier and Sam Clay as they create a comic about a Nazi-fighting superhero, while also grappling with Hitler's reign of terror.

Losing Earth
Nathaniel Rich
Nathaniel Rich talks the reader through the general awareness of climate change since the 70s, and all the ways in which people fought for change and, equally, the ways in which we didn't succeed.

Why I'm No Longer Talking to White People About Race
Reni Eddo-Lodge
An exploration of what it's like to be a person of colour in Britain today, discussing everything from whitewashed feminism and class to the history of slavery and racism in the UK.

It's Not About the Burqa
Mariam Khan
Seventeen frank pieces of writing from Muslim women about a wide variety of topics, from love to feminism, sex, queer identity and faith.

Bad Feminist
Roxane Gay
A selection of insightful essays, commenting on feminism today.

The Uninhabitable Earth
David Wallace-Wells
Exploring the consequences of rising temperatures, one degree at a time, David Wallace-Wells paints a sobering image of what the changing climate has in store for humanity, and what needs to be done to prevent it.

The Good Immigrant
Nikesh Shukla
A collection of stories from 21 Black, Asian and minority ethnic voices from across Britain.

The Girl Who Smiled Beads
Clemantine Wamariya and Elizabeth Weil
The memoir of Clemantine, who left Rwanda with her sister and spent six years wandering through seven African countries, trying to find a safe place to live, eventually ending up in the United States to build a new life.

Stim: An Autistic Anthology
Lizzie Huxley-Jones
A series of stories, illustrations and essays from a range of autistic voices, championing often unheard perspectives and experiences.

We Crossed a Bridge and It Trembled
Wendy Pearlman
A collection of wartime testimonies and written fragments from a variety of Syrians who have been affected by the war.

The New Jim Crow
Michelle Alexander
In this work civil rights litigator and legal scholar Michelle Alexander explains the way the US criminal justice system is used to enforce racial discrimination and oppression.

The Yellow Wallpaper
Charlotte Perkins Gilman
A chilling short story about a woman who starts seeing things appear in the wallpaper of the room she's confined to.

Three Shadows
Cyril Pedrosa
When three shadows appear outside the house of a young family, the family embarks on a journey in an attempt to flee death. A touching and haunting graphic novel.

The Ice Palace
Tarjei Vesaas
Be transported to the snowy landscape of Norway by this lyrical and classic masterpiece, which features the disappearance of a young girl.

Ghachar Ghochar
Vivek Shanbhag
When a family's fortune takes an upturn, their relationships start changing and falling apart.

The Lottery and Other Stories
Shirley Jackson
A series of terrifying short stories, including the world-famous "The Lottery", first published in *The New Yorker* in 1948, horrifying readers at the time.

Of Mice and Men
John Steinbeck
A well-known classic that packs an emotional punch, following two drifters as they search for work in California's Salinas Valley.

Women and Power
Mary Beard
How does history treat powerful women? Mary Beard reflects on topics from consent to misogyny and Homer to Hillary Clinton in this manifesto.

The Bloody Chamber and Other Stories
Angela Carter
This Gothic short story collection is a dark spin on the fairy tales and legends we think we know.

A Portable Shelter
Kirsty Logan
Two women on an island tell stories to their unborn baby, while keeping the storytelling a secret from each other.

Pet
Akwaeke Emezi
People believe monsters don't exist anymore, but Jam knows this isn't true. A powerful and original story dealing with a wide range of social issues.

Dumplin'
Julie Murphy
Filled with friendship, family and lots
of Dolly Parton references, discover
the story of Willowdean Dickson's out-
of-character decision to enter the Miss
Clover City beauty pageant, making
a statement that a fat girl belongs there
as much as anyone else.

Daisy Jones and The Six
Taylor Jenkins Reid
No-one knows why the famous band
Daisy Jones and The Six split in 1979,
until now...

The Lido
Libby Page
A tender story about a young reporter
with anxiety who is writing a story about
the closing of a local pool. Then she
meets 86-year-old widow Rosemary, who
would lose lots of important memories
if the pool were to close.

Love in a Cold Climate
Nancy Mitford
A romantic comedy set in England
between the wars, featuring plenty
of glamour, expectations and secrets.

The Hitchhiker's Guide to the Galaxy
Douglas Adams
When Arthur Dent gets rescued from
Earth seconds before it's destroyed,
he embarks on a hilarious and madcap
journey through the galaxy with a wild
bunch of fellow travellers, including
Marvin, the depressed robot.

Get a Life, Chloe Brown
Talia Hibbert
Chloe Brown, a chronically ill computer
geek, enlists the help of bad boy Redford
"Red" Morgan to rebel and change up her
life, following a near-death experience.

Where'd You Go, Bernadette
Maria Semple
When Bernadette Fox disappears after
being on the brink of a meltdown, her
family is left to pick up the pieces.

Heartstopper
Alice Oseman
See the anxious and openly gay Charlie
and rugby player Nick slowly fall in love
in this adorable and absolutely
heartwarming graphic novel.

When Dimple Met Rishi
Sandhya Menon
Dimple Shah knows what she wants
for her future. Rishi Patel is a hopeless
romantic and his parents think Dimple
would be the perfect match for him.
Then they meet at a summer programme
for aspiring web developers. Will these
opposites clash...?

Eleanor Oliphant Is Completely Fine
Gail Honeyman
Eleanor Oliphant struggles with fitting
in and spends all her weekends alone.
Then she befriends Raymond, the IT guy
from her office, as they help an elderly
gentleman who's been in an accident,
and her life starts to change.

The Handmaid's Tale
Margaret Atwood
As relevant now as when it was published in 1985, this classic of the genre is set in the Republic of Gilead, where fertile women are forced to be Handmaids who carry the children of high-ranking members of society.

Never Let Me Go
Kazuo Ishiguro
A gentle and haunting novel, told by a young woman who looks back on her time at Hailsham, which seems like a normal English boarding school, but has many secrets to hide.

The Day of the Triffids
John Wyndham
A 1950s sci-fi classic, which starts with the iconic scene of its protagonist wandering through the abandoned streets of London, after most of society goes blind and triffids, a strange breed of moving plants, take over.

The Water Cure
Sophie Mackintosh
Reminiscent of *The Virgin Suicides*, this novel will leave the reader with many questions, while also sucking them into the world of three sisters on an isolated island, raised to fear men.

We
Yevgeny Zamyatin
The Russian classic that influenced a huge variety of sci-fi authors, set in a totalitarian society where one person comes to discover they have a soul.

Station Eleven
Emily St John Mandel
A surprisingly hopeful pandemic story, following a troupe of nomadic actors and musicians, known as the Travelling Symphony, 20 years after the outbreak of the mysterious Georgian Flu.

Fahrenheit 451
Ray Bradbury
Guy Montag, a fireman whose job it is to start fires and destroy books, slowly starts to question the rules of his world after meeting his young neighbour Clarisse.

Annihilation
Jeff VanderMeer
Join the twelfth expedition, a group of four women, as they enter Area X, which has been isolated for decades and has claimed the lives of all previous research expeditions.

Woman on the Edge of Time
Marge Piercy
Consuelo Ramos is shown both a utopian and a dystopian society by a person time-travelling from the year 2137, while being unjustly committed to a mental hospital in New York.

Blindness
José Saramago
When a pandemic that causes blindness strikes, a group of terrified victims is confined to an empty mental hospital.

A Monster Calls
Patrick Ness
While worrying about his mother's
illness, Conor is visited at night by
an ancient creature, who demands
to know "the truth". An extraordinary
tale accompanied by stunning and
dark illustrations.

We Are Okay
Nina LaCour
A quiet, gentle and beautiful Young Adult
novel about Marin, who is spending the
winter break in an empty dorm. When Mabel
comes to visit, Marin has to let memories
of the past slowly come back to her.

H Is for Hawk
Helen Macdonald
A mix of nature writing and memoir
about the sudden death of Helen's father,
her love of hawks and so much more.

How Do You Like Me Now?
Holly Bourne
Tori is pretending to have it all together:
the successful career, the long-term
relationship, a great best friend. But the
truth is, she doesn't know what the future
looks like for her. A funny and confronting
picture of a woman in her 30s.

Clap When You Land
Elizabeth Acevedo
A novel in verse dealing with grief, as two
girls in different worlds come to terms with
the loss of their father in a plane crash.

Grief Is the Thing with Feathers
Max Porter
This is a tale you won't forget very easily.
While a father and his two young sons try
to come to terms with the death of their
wife and mother, they are visited by a
crow, who will stay until they no longer
need him.

Almost Love
Louise O'Neill
Sarah is in an all-consuming relationship
with the older and successful Matthew,
and her friends and family are worried
for her. Is love supposed to hurt like this?

A Heartbreaking Work of Staggering Genius
Dave Eggers
The critically acclaimed memoir about
Dave's life with his siblings, after his
parents die from cancer and he takes
on the responsibility of looking after
his younger brother, Toph.

The Discomfort of Evening
Marieke Lucas Rijneveld
A Dutch bestseller set in a small town,
about a tragic accident and sudden death
of a younger brother, narrated by a sister
living in her own world.

The Truth About Keeping Secrets
Savannah Brown
When Sydney's dad, a psychiatrist in a
small Ohio town, unexpectedly dies in
car crash, Sydney becomes obsessed with
finding out what happened. And why did
June, the homecoming queen, show up
at his funeral?

I'll Be Gone in the Dark
Michelle McNamara
A true-crime account of the Golden State Killer, who had California in his power for years. This book also finally gives a voice to his countless victims. Guaranteed to keep you up at night.

Lullaby
Leïla Slimani
A young Parisian couple think that they've found the perfect babysitter for their children, but the more they spend time together, the more the relationship sours.

My Sister, the Serial Killer
Oyinkan Braithwaite
Sinister and funny, detailing the misadventures of two sisters, one of whom can't seem to stop murdering her boyfriends. But when Ayoola moves on to the next boyfriend and starts dating Korede's crush, the situation gets even more complicated.

Through the Woods
Emily Carroll
Five chilling short stories in graphic novel form, inspired by fairy tales, folklore and the Gothic, with illustrations in stunning colours and terrifying characters.

Ninth House
Leigh Bardugo
A book filled with secret societies, ghosts, power and magic, set in the dark hallways of Yale.

We Have Always Lived in the Castle
Shirley Jackson
Merricat lives with only her sister Constance and Uncle Julian, because the rest of her family is dead. People in the town whisper about what happened in their mansion, and the mystery starts to unfold when a visitor arrives.

The Secret History
Donna Tartt
This modern classic follows five students at a New England college, who slowly lose touch with reality after a horrific chain of events. Dark and irresistibly compelling.

Gone Girl
Gillian Flynn
What happened to beautiful, perfect Amy? When she disappears on her fifth wedding anniversary and her husband Nick is suspected to be involved, it's slowly revealed that nothing is as it seems.

Frankenstein
Mary Shelley
Written in 1818, this classic will surprise any reader who thinks they know what they're in for. The Gothic tale of Victor Frankenstein who wants to create life and designs a creature who, after being rejected, sets out for revenge.

The Seven Deaths of Evelyn Hardcastle
Stuart Turton
A mind-bending whodunit with a character who keeps waking up in the body of a different guest at Blackheath Manor, where a murder has taken place.

The Overstory
Richard Powers
Discover a ring of interconnected stories, covering a wide variety of times and locations, all relating to the natural world and the way people experience it.

The Salt Path
Raynor Winn
A couple decides to walk 630 miles of the English coast after discovering the husband is terminally ill and losing everything they have. A story about grief, loss, nature and the meaning of home.

Where the Crawdads Sing
Delia Owens
A heartbreaking coming-of-age story, set in a quiet town in Northern California and in the marsh where Kya Clark has lived by herself for years. Kya's life starts changing after a local is found dead and the police suspect her.

Entangled Life
Merlin Sheldrake
An exploration of the weird and wonderful world of fungi, which are connected to many more things than we might expect.

Far from the Madding Crowd
Thomas Hardy
When the young and independent Bathsheba Everdene starts her position as the farmer of a large estate, she quickly becomes surrounded by three suitors who in different ways affect her life and the community around her. Featuring gorgeous descriptions of rural life.

The Summer Book
Tove Jansson
By the author of the Moomins books, and inspired by some of her own experiences, this is the story of an artist and her young granddaughter who spend a summer together on a small island in Finland.

The Shepherd's Life
James Rebanks
Coming from a long line of shepherds in the Lake District, James Rebanks describes the beauty and hardships of his work through the seasons.

Two Trees Make a Forest
Jessica J Lee
Jessica J Lee starts a journey through Taiwan to discover the history of her family, who moved from China, to Taiwan and then to Canada.

The Grassling
Elizabeth-Jane Burnett
A celebration and exploration of our roots and how the land shapes us, in the wake of the author's father declining health and his connection to a small village in Devon.

Underland
Robert Macfarlane
Dive into the surface of our planet, as Robert Macfarlane explores the Earth's underworlds through literature, memory and nature.

Anne of Green Gables
Lucy Maud Montgomery
The beloved Canadian classic, about
an energetic and imaginative orphan girl
who unexpectedly finds a home at the
farm of Marilla and Matthew Cuthbert.

Matilda
Roald Dahl
Follow the young, but incredibly smart
Matilda as she uses her wit and talent for
practical jokes to deal with the bullies in
her life, including the nightmarish school
principal Miss Trunchbull, and fights for
a life she deserves.

The Moomins
Tove Jansson
A classic Swedish series about the
adventures of an eccentric family of troll
characters who live in Moominvalley.

A Series of Unfortunate Events
Lemony Snicket
Meet the ill-fated Baudelaire orphans,
who are placed in the custody of their evil
relative Count Olaf after their parents die
in a fire. A series of books filled with
Gothic tones and dark humour, but also
a lot of heart and plenty of puns.

Holes
Louis Sachar
Bad luck has followed Stanley Yelnats
and his family for a long time, causing
him to end up at Camp Green Lake, a
juvenile correction centre where all the
boys have to dig a big hole every day to
improve their character. But is there
something more to this assignment?

I Capture the Castle
Dodie Smith
The journal of 17-year-old Cassandra,
about her life in a crumbling castle with
her eccentric and impoverished family.
Their lives are forever changed when the
American heirs to the castle arrive.

Howl's Moving Castle
Diana Wynne Jones
The young Sophie becomes the victim
of a spell by the Witch of the Waste,
who turns her into an old lady. Her only
chance of breaking the spell can be found
in the Wizard Howl's moving castle.

The House on Mango Street
Sandra Cisneros
The story of a young Latina girl growing
up in the Hispanic quarter of Chicago,
as she's starting to figure out who she
wants to become.

A Wrinkle in Time
Madeleine L'Engle
A classic sci-fi adventure in which a group
of kids go looking for Charles' scientist
father who is lost in time and space.

Northern Lights
Philip Pullman
The first in the *His Dark Materials* trilogy
follows the adventures of the young
and wild Lyra, who grew up at Oxford
University with her animal daemon
always by her side.

Don't Call Us Dead
Danez Smith
In this award-winning and moving collection Danez Smith tackles topics from police brutality to HIV.

Night Sky with Exit Wounds
Ocean Vuong
A stunning debut about the Vietnamese-American experience, with themes of memory, love and grief.

The Girl Aquarium
Jen Campbell
A bold and mesmerizing collection about girls, bodies, nature, beauty and fairy tales.

Even This Page Is White
Vivek Shraya
Vivek Shraya's poems about race, gender and pop culture will draw you in and surprise you.

Brand New Ancients
Kae Tempest
This unique combination of storytelling, poetry and rap tells the story of two families, against the backdrop of classical mythology.

Set Me on Fire
Ella Risbridger
An anthology with a poem for every kind of reader and every kind of feeling, from poets both alive and dead.

North
Seamus Heaney
Poetry drawing on the Northern European experience, from Irish identity and landscape to Scandinavian and English invasions, by the world-famous Nobel Prize winner.

My Life Had Stood a Loaded Gun
Emily Dickinson
This Penguin Little Black Classic is a fantastic introduction to one of America's greatest writers, featuring poems about death, isolation and beauty.

The Black Unicorn
Audre Lorde
Audre Lord's most acclaimed poetry collection, mixing identity, motherhood, magic, female strength and so much more.

Life on Mars
Tracy K Smith
The perfect poetry collection for lovers of sci-fi and filled with pop culture references, by the United States' 22nd Poetry Laureate.

Outlander
Diana Gabaldon
Travel through time from 1945 to 1743 in Scotland, as former combat nurse Claire Randall is accidentally transported through an ancient standing stone, after which she's thrown together with a young Scottish warrior called Jamie Fraser.

Like Water for Chocolate
Laura Esquivel
A magical and bittersweet tale of a family in Mexico, including a forbidden love, a wedding and lots of food.

Aristotle and Dante Discover the Secrets of the Universe
Benjamin Alire Sáenz
After opposites Aristotle and Dante meet at a local pool, they start spending more time together. A touching story exploring sexuality, love and identity.

Red, White and Royal Blue
Casey McQuiston
Staging a fake friendship between the English Prince Henry and the American First Son Alex Claremont-Diaz seemed like a good idea to help American–British relations, with the unexpected consequence that they start a secret relationship.

Pride and Prejudice
Jane Austen
This Austen novel is a surefire pick for any romance recommendation. Featuring a hate to love story between the opinionated Elizabeth Bennet and the stubborn and rich Mr Darcy, set in Regency England.

Sofia Khan Is Not Obliged
Ayisha Malik
When Sofia Khan is asked by her boss to write a book about the Muslim dating scene she hesitantly accepts. She'll need all the help she can get when she goes in search of stories, and happens to find her own.

Love in the Time of Cholera
Gabriel García Márquez
Florentino Ariza is heartbroken when the young woman he's in love with marries a rich doctor. But when her husband dies, he knows this is his chance to finally get it right.

Call Me By Your Name
André Aciman
A powerful romance story of an adolescent boy and a summer guest who meet in the Italian Riviera. From seeming indifference to passion, this is an unforgettable story.

This Is How You Lose the Time War
Amal El-Mohtar and Max Gladstone
This time-travel novella features a love story between two female agents who are each trying to fight for survival. But there is a war going on and if their relationship comes to light, it could mean the end for both of them.

The Time Traveler's Wife
Audrey Niffenegger
The moving story of Clare, an art student, and Henry, a librarian, who get to know each other and fall in love. Meanwhile Henry constantly finds himself misplaced in time, meeting Clare at different points in her life.

Washington Black
Esi Edugyan
Journey along the eastern coast of America and to the Arctic, with explorer and abolitionist Christopher Wilde and the 11-year-old manservant Washington Black, who invents a new life for himself.

The Five
Hallie Rubenhold
Discover the story of "the Ripper" from an entirely different point of view. This portrait of the five women who were killed by Jack the Ripper gives an enlightening and human insight into the daily life of Victorian Londoners.

Kindred
Octavia E Butler
One day, an African-American woman finds herself pulled through time to pre-Civil War America, where she helps save a drowning white boy who turns out to be one of her ancestors. This impactful time-travel novel tackles power dynamics, racism and gender issues.

The Miniaturist
Jessie Burton
In 17th-century Amsterdam an 18-year-old bride receives a cabinet-sized replica of her home which starts to mirror her own life, as she tries to uncover the secrets of the household.

The Bass Rock
Evie Wyld
Follow the intertwined lives of three women, one living in the 1700s, one just after the Second World War and the third a few decades later, through a witch persecution, new husbands and mourning.

The Confessions of Frannie Langton
Sara Collins
Set in Georgian London and on a Jamaican sugar plantation, this is the story of Frannie Langton, who is accused of the murder of her employers.

The Assault
Harry Mulisch
During the winter of 1945 in occupied Netherlands, a Nazi collaborator is killed on his way home. A 12-year-old boy is the only survivor of the German retaliation that follows. As he tries to live a normal life, the past keeps following him.

The Doll Factory
Elizabeth Macneal
When Iris is asked to model for pre-Raphaelite artist Louis Frost, she requests painting lessons in return. A tale of obsession and art, set against the backdrop of the 1850 Great Exhibition in London.

The Essex Serpent
Sarah Perry
Widow and amateur naturalist Cora Seaborne travels to Essex with her son Francis, looking for a new start. As rumours about the mysterious Essex Serpent appear, Cora strikes up a relationship with the local vicar.

Wolf Hall
Hilary Mantel
This rich novel and Man Booker Prize-winner chronicles the story of Thomas Cromwell in 1520s England, during Henry VIII's tumultuous reign.

Emma
Jane Austen
Perhaps the Austen novel that divides readers the most, featuring the rich and spoiled Emma Woodhouse, who can't help but meddle in the lives of the people that she meets.

Normal People
Sally Rooney
Set in Ireland, this story chronicles how popular Connell and shy Marianne are drawn together and break apart, at school and later at Trinity College. A story about love, family and class.

Little Women
Louisa May Alcott
A well-loved classic about the four very different March sisters and their journey growing up, discovering love, death, responsibility and so much more.

To All the Boys I Loved Before
Jenny Han
When Lara Jean's sister sends out all the secret letters she's written to her past and current crushes, her life suddenly becomes a lot more complicated…and exciting.

Rebecca
Daphne du Maurier
A Gothic novel about a young woman who marries a rich widower, and discovers that his life is still haunted by his previous wife, Rebecca.

The Kite Runner
Khaled Hosseini
The heartbreaking story about an unlikely friendship between two boys, with the history of Afghanistan playing out at the same time.

Hidden Figures
Margot Lee Shetterly
Discover the story of the female African-American mathematicians, also known as "human computers", who played a vital role in NASA's space programme.

Room
Emma Donoghue
Five-year-old Jack has only ever known one room, which is his entire universe. But then his Ma comes up with a plan to escape from the place where she's been held captive for seven years, and their entire world changes.

Big Little Lies
Liane Moriarty
Murder, secrets and seemingly perfect lives are the heart of this novel, where three women come together.

Dune
Frank Herbert
When a noble family that was put in charge of ruling a bleak planet is betrayed, a young heir is forced to go on a journey and fulfil his destiny.

Dracula
Bram Stoker
The classic Gothic tale of Count Dracula, as he tries to move from his castle in Transylvania to England in order to find new victims.

Beloved
Toni Morrison
Eighteen years ago Sethe escaped from slavery in Ohio, but her mind is still haunted by the past and the ghost of her baby.

Nineteen Eighty-Four
George Orwell
A political satire and dystopian classic featuring a bureaucratic world without any individuality, where its citizens are constantly observed. Orwell predicted many inventions and discussions that still occupy us to this day.

Brideshead Revisited
Evelyn Waugh
Set during the run-up to the Second World War, this nostalgic novel covers the Marchmains and their rapidly disappearing world of privilege.

Orlando
Virginia Woolf
Taking place across three centuries, this novel examines the nature of sexuality. Orlando starts the novel as a young nobleman and ends it as an adult woman, all while witnessing history.

Wuthering Heights
Emily Brontë
A Gothic doomed love story, filled with obsession and hauntings, set in the Yorkshire Moors.

The Great Gatsby
F Scott Fitzgerald
This tale of the Jazz Age and America in the 1920s is frequently read in schools and an intriguing story to revisit.

Invisible Man
Ralph Ellison
Published in 1952, *Invisible Man* follows a protagonist without a name, as he travels from the Deep South to Harlem and beyond, discussing and showcasing bigotry and the racial divide.

The Bell Jar
Sylvia Plath
As she starts an internship at a New York fashion magazine, Esther finds her life slipping out of control as she deals with depression.

Giovanni's Room
James Baldwin
A haunting novel and a classic of gay literature, set in 1950s Paris.

Parable of the Sower
Octavia E Butler
It's 2025 and the outlook of the world is bleak, as people are plagued by water shortages, disease and war. When young Lauren's family is killed and her home is destroyed, she is forced to join an endless stream of desperate people on the road.

Asking For It
Louise O'Neill
This incredibly relevant and chilling novel shows the aftermath of the sexual assault of a teenage girl at a party in a small town in Ireland.

Such a Fun Age
Kiley Reid
Discussions about racism, class and performative allyship are central in this novel that starts with a young Black woman who is almost arrested in a grocery store while babysitting a little white girl.

Extremely Loud and Incredibly Close
Jonathan Safran Foer
When nine-year-old Oskar's father is killed in the 9/11 attacks, Oskar tries to figure out the mystery behind a key in his father's closet, which causes him to come across a wide variety of strangers.

There There
Tommy Orange
Follow the intertwined lives of 12 characters from Native communities, who are all travelling to the Big Oakland Powwow.

Autumn
Ali Smith
This first instalment in the beautiful Seasonal Quartet of incredibly relevant stories focuses on themes of art, harvest, Brexit and immigration.

The Hate U Give
Angie Thomas
This Young Adult novel, inspired by the Black Lives Matter movement, follows a teenage girl who witnesses her unarmed friend being fatally shot by a police officer. Now it's up to her to decide if she will remain silent, or speak up.

On Earth We're Briefly Gorgeous
Ocean Vuong
A stunning portrait of family, roots and the power of storytelling, written as a letter from a son to a mother who can't read.

Noughts and Crosses
Malorie Blackman
In a world of Crosses (dark-skinned and holding most of the power) and Noughts (a white minority living without privilege and with limited opportunities), two star-crossed lovers, who have been friends since they were young, step right into danger.

So You've Been Publicly Shamed
Jon Ronson
A funny and incredibly interesting book documenting people who have been at the centre of social media outrages and the part we all play in them.

Homegoing
Yaa Gyasi
A multi-generational story that starts
with two half-sisters, one who is sent
to the United States on a slave ship and
one who marries a slave trader and
remains in Ghana.

One Hundred Years of Solitude
Gabriel García Márquez
A mix of fantasy and reality, wars, politics
and magical realism, this masterpiece
tells the story of seven generations of the
Buendía family and the town they built.

The Vanishing Half
Brit Bennett
The story of identical twin sisters who,
once they grow up, go on to live entirely
different lives. What will happen when
the future of their families is destined
to connect again?

Little Fires Everywhere
Celeste Ng
Everything seems perfect in Shaker
Heights. When Mia Warren arrives with
her teenage daughter Pearl, their lives
and those of the Richardsons become
intertwined and start a chain of events
and mysteries.

The Dutch House
Ann Patchett
When Cyril Conroy brings his family
from poverty into wealth, the first thing
they do is buy a lavish estate outside
Philadelphia, called the Dutch House.
This is unfortunately the start of a dark
path downwards.

Girl, Woman, Other
Bernadine Evaristo
You'll meet 12 different characters in this
stunning and vibrant novel about modern
Britain and Black womanhood.

The Namesake
Jhumpa Lahiri
Focusing on the immigrant experience
and the clash between generations,
The Namesake follows a family from
their life in Calcutta to their new life
in Massachusetts.

Pachinko
Min Jin Lee
Korean Sunja falls in love with a wealthy
stranger and becomes pregnant. When
she finds out she's been lied to, she
marries another man instead and starts
a new life in Japan. The novel tracks the
life of Sunja, her sons and all the people
that connect them and tear them apart.

We Were Liars
E Lockhart
A suspenseful and lyrical story of a
wealthy family and all its secrets. Set on
a private island and filled with allusions
to *King Lear*, this is a Young Adult classic
you won't forget soon.

How to Be Both
Ali Smith
A novel that can be read in two ways, all
about art, love and injustice, set in both
the 1460s and the 1960s.

Reading wish list

_____
_____
_____
_____
_____
_____
_____
_____
_____
_____
_____
_____
_____
_____
_____
_____
_____
_____
_____
_____
_____
_____

Book loan tracker

Title	Lent to	Date

Title	Borrowed from	Date

First published in Great Britain in 2021
by Mitchell Beazley, an imprint of
Octopus Publishing Group Ltd
Carmelite House
50 Victoria Embankment
London EC4Y 0DZ
www.octopusbooks.co.uk
www.octopusbooksusa.com

An Hachette UK Company
www.hachette.co.uk

Distributed in the US by
Hachette Book Group
1290 Avenue of the Americas
4th and 5th Floors
New York, NY 10104

Distributed in Canada by
Canadian Manda Group
664 Annette St.
Toronto, Ontario, Canada M6S 2C8

ISBN 978-1-78472-749-9

A CIP catalogue record for this book is
available from the British Library.

Printed and bound in China

10 9 8 7 6 5 4 3 2 1

Publisher: Alison Starling
Project Editor: Emily Brickell
Art Director: Juliette Norsworthy
Illustrator: Agnes Bicocchi
Senior Production Controller: Emily Noto